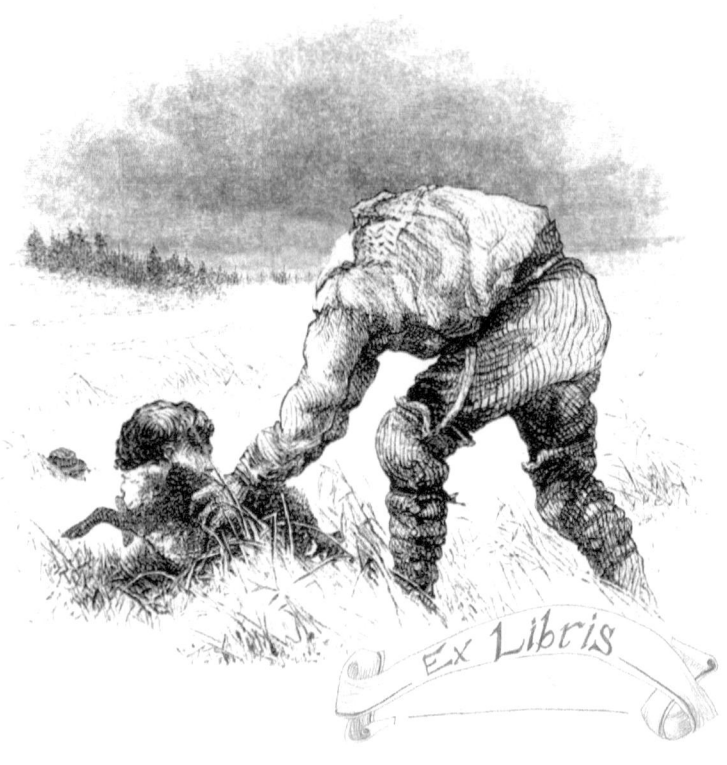

Printed in the United States of America

First Edition, 2016

ISBN-10: 0-9910466-4-1
ISBN-13: 978-0-9910466-4-5

A. Keck Press
New York, New York

Riddled
with
Spots

S. ZAR & WHYMPER

1

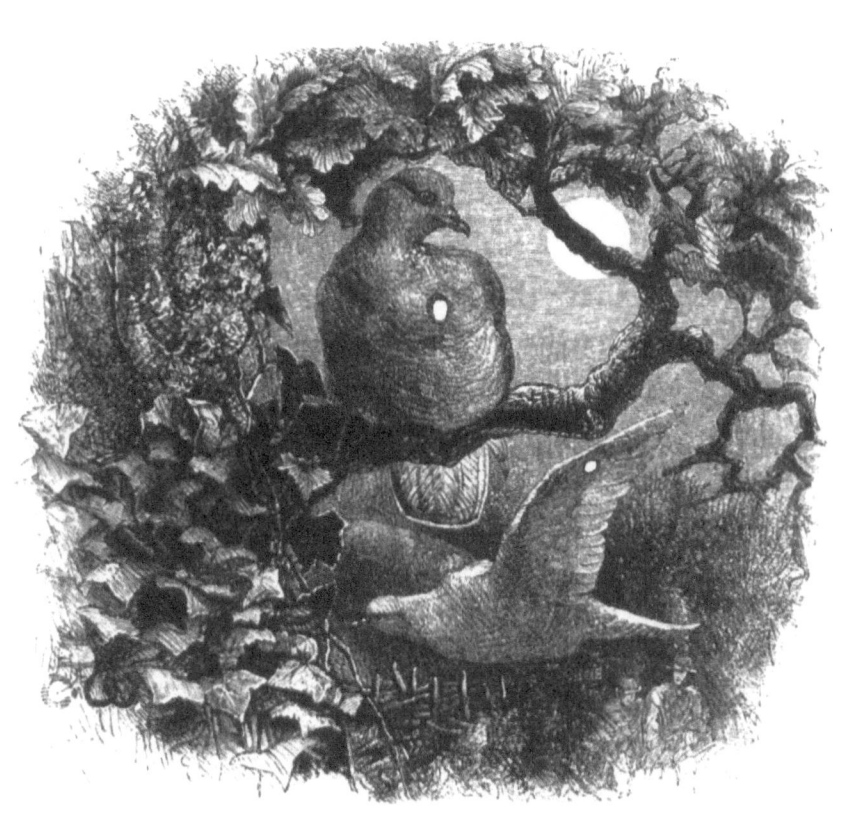

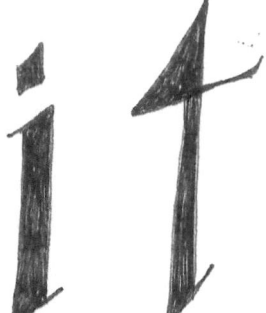

It is a mystery to him.

He approaches.

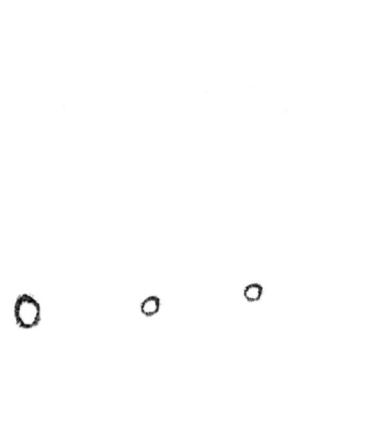

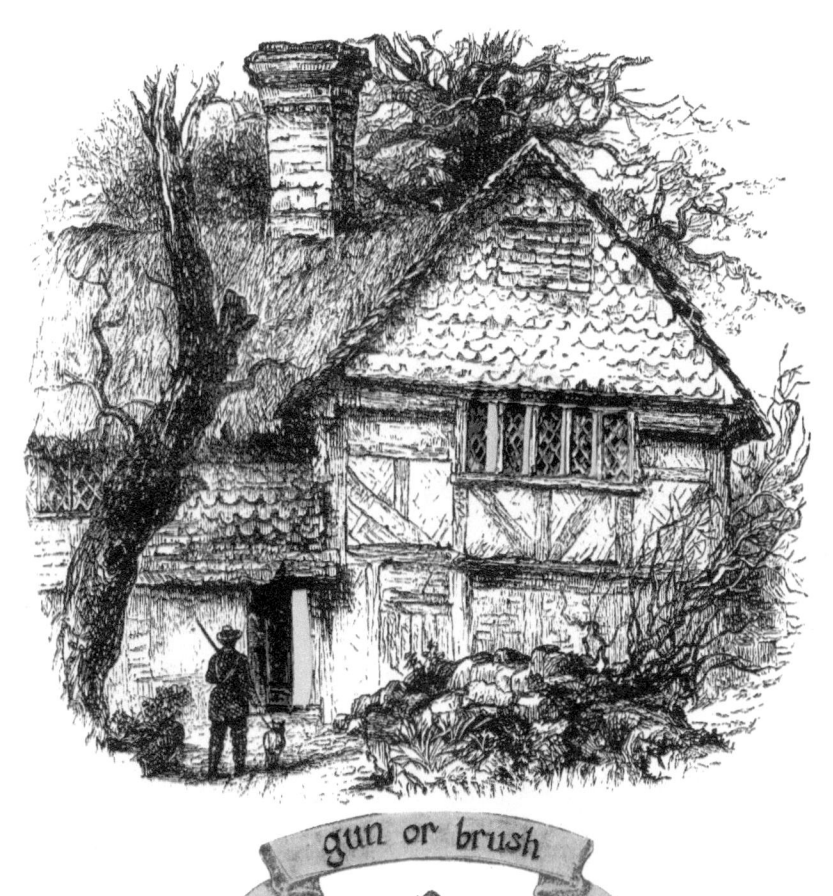

gun or brush

?

He learns to be still.

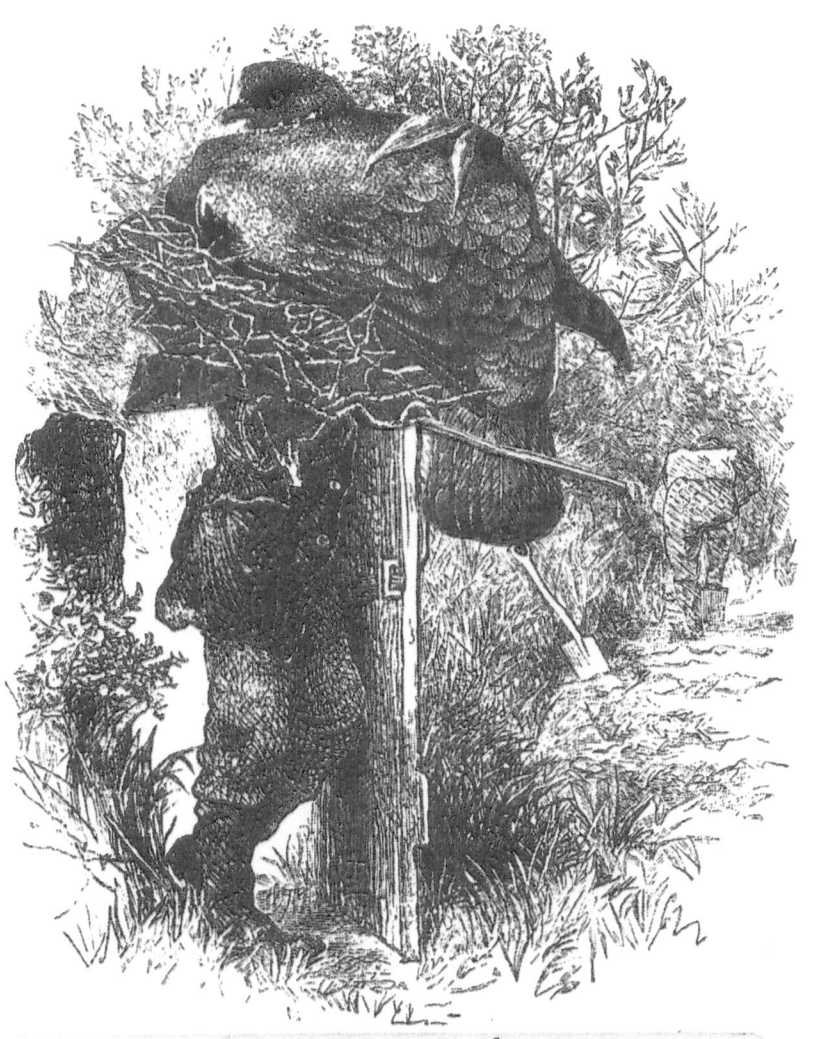

Still

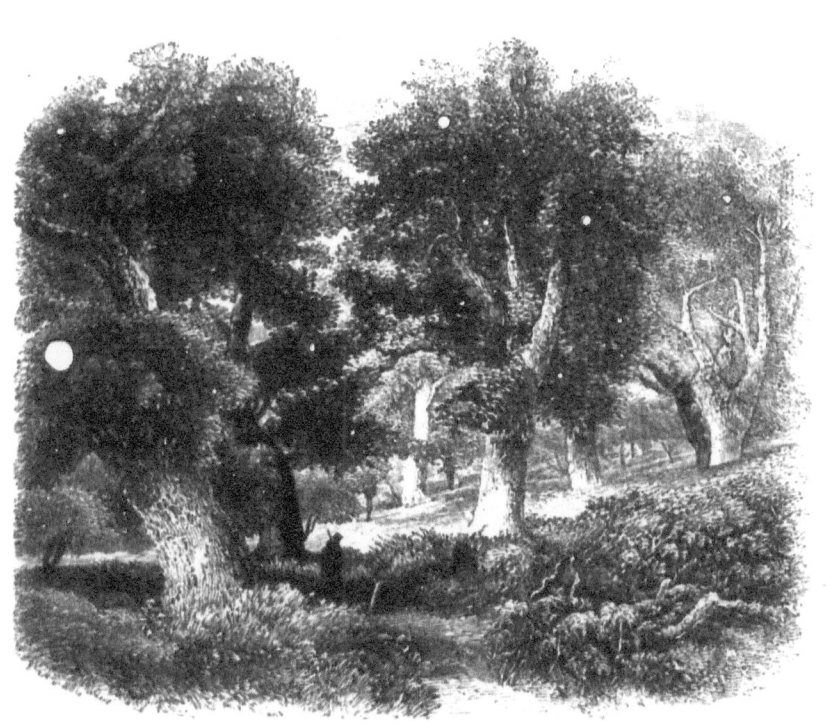

If you blink you might miss it.

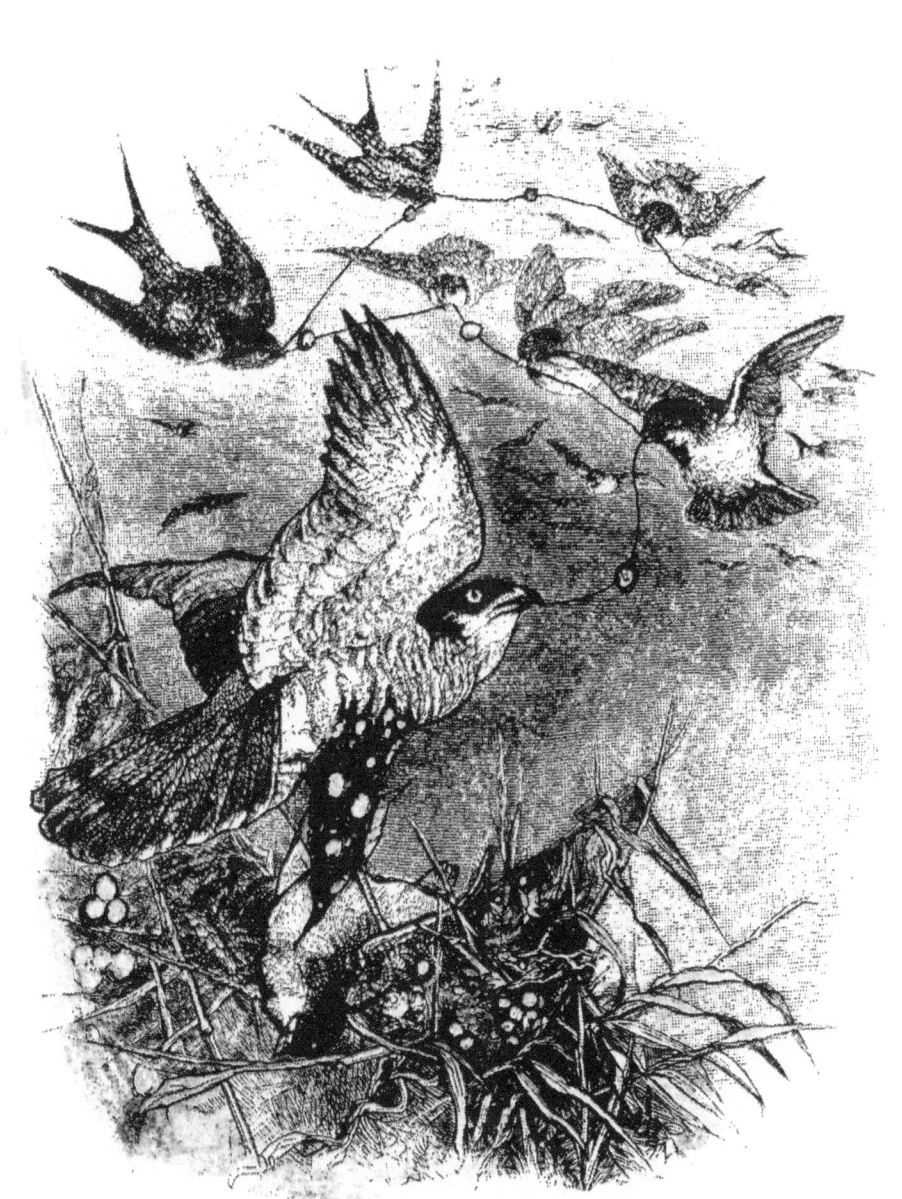

2

This hunt has changed him somehow.

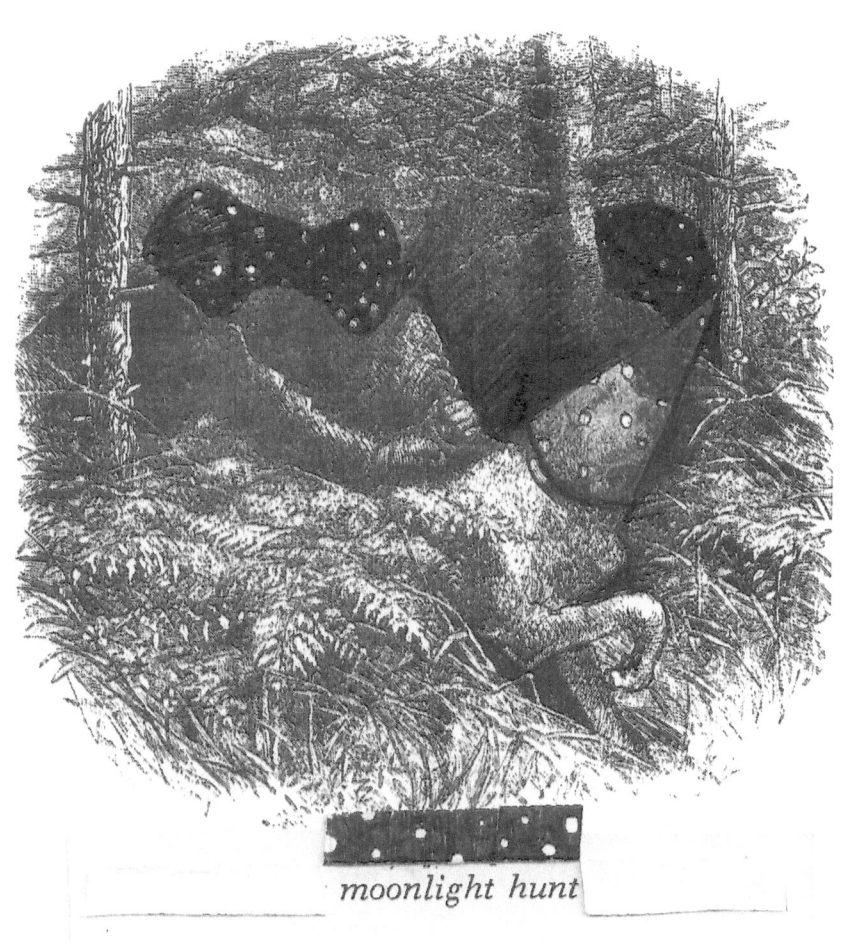

moonlight hunt

Even at rest, he asks questions.

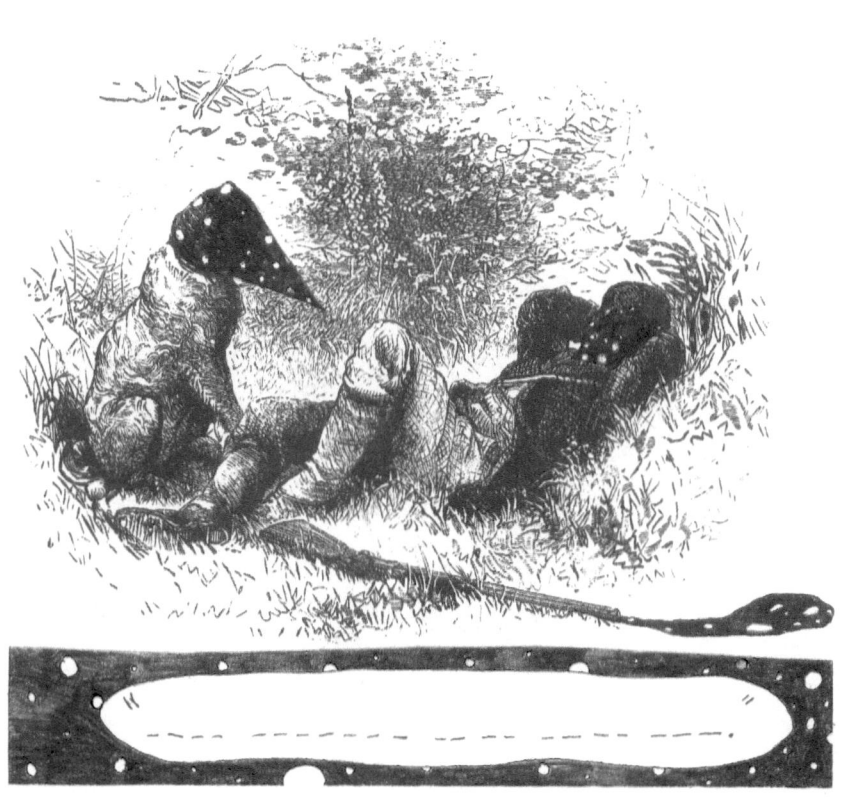

He is not alone.

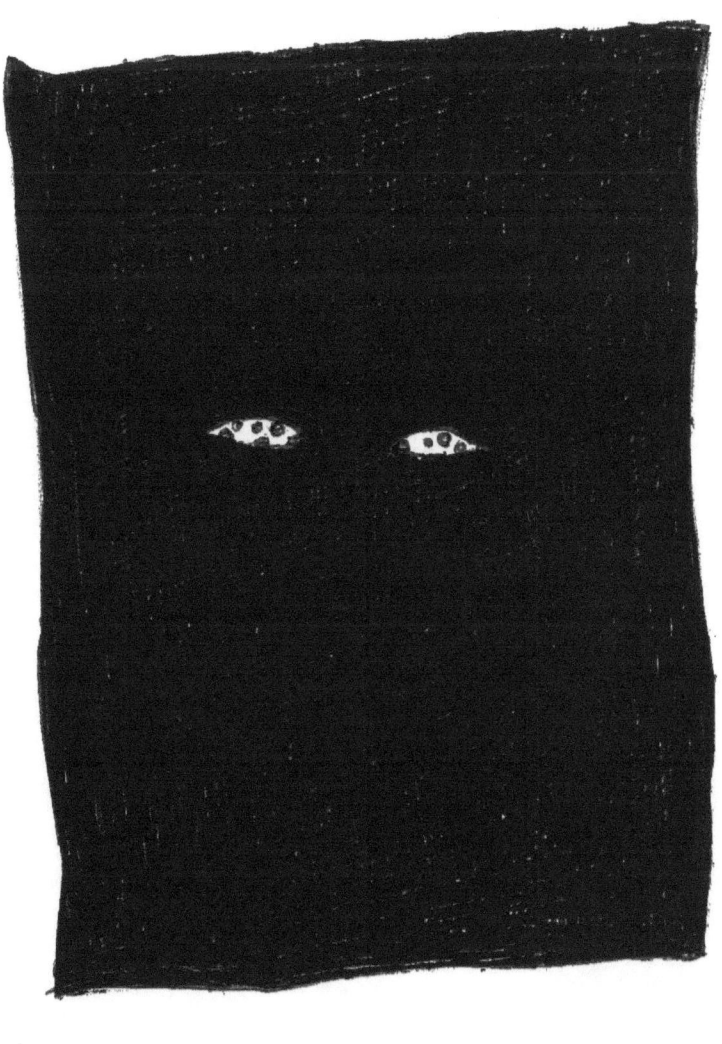

Look well
to each step

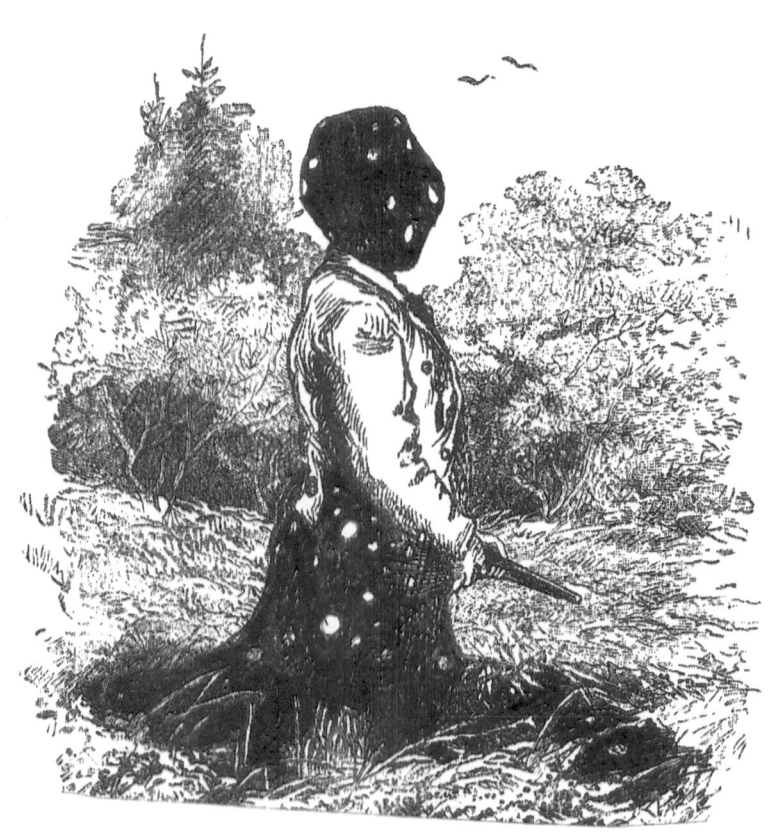

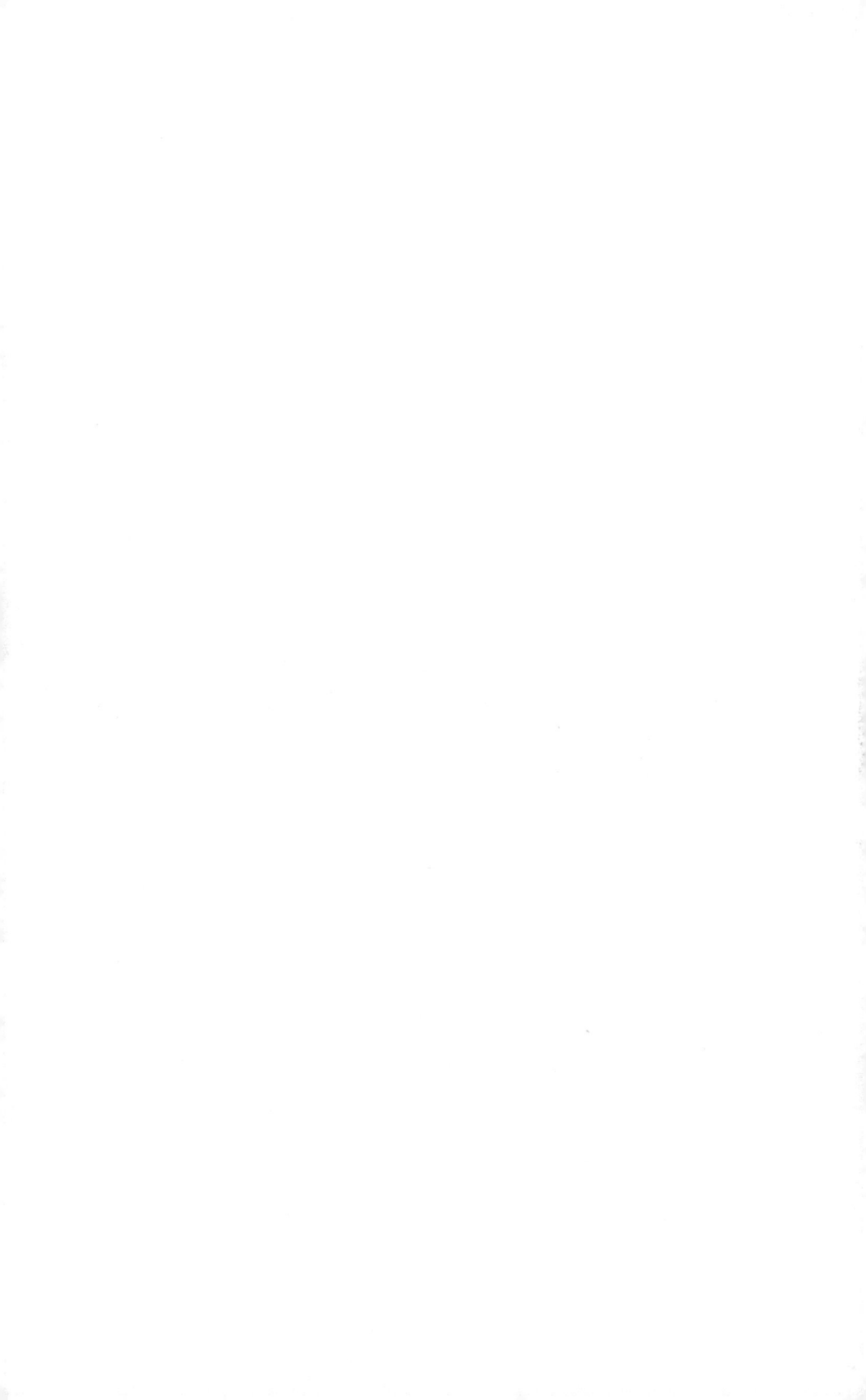

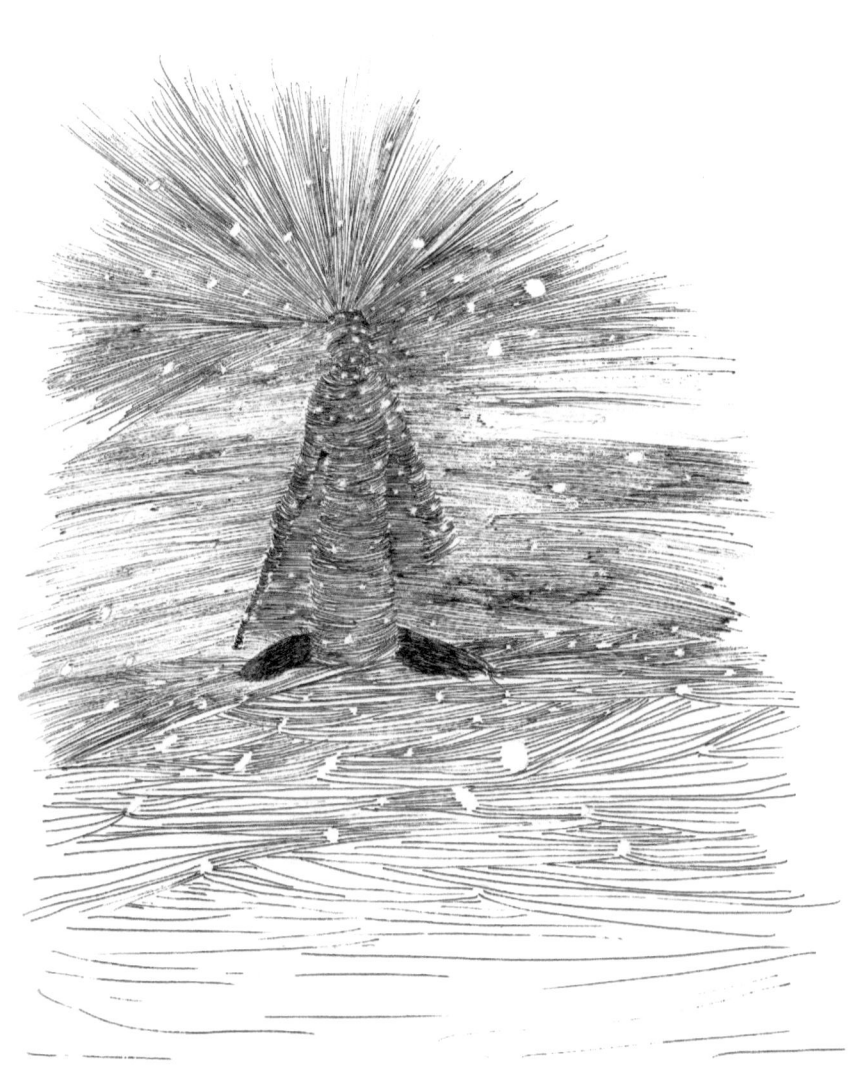

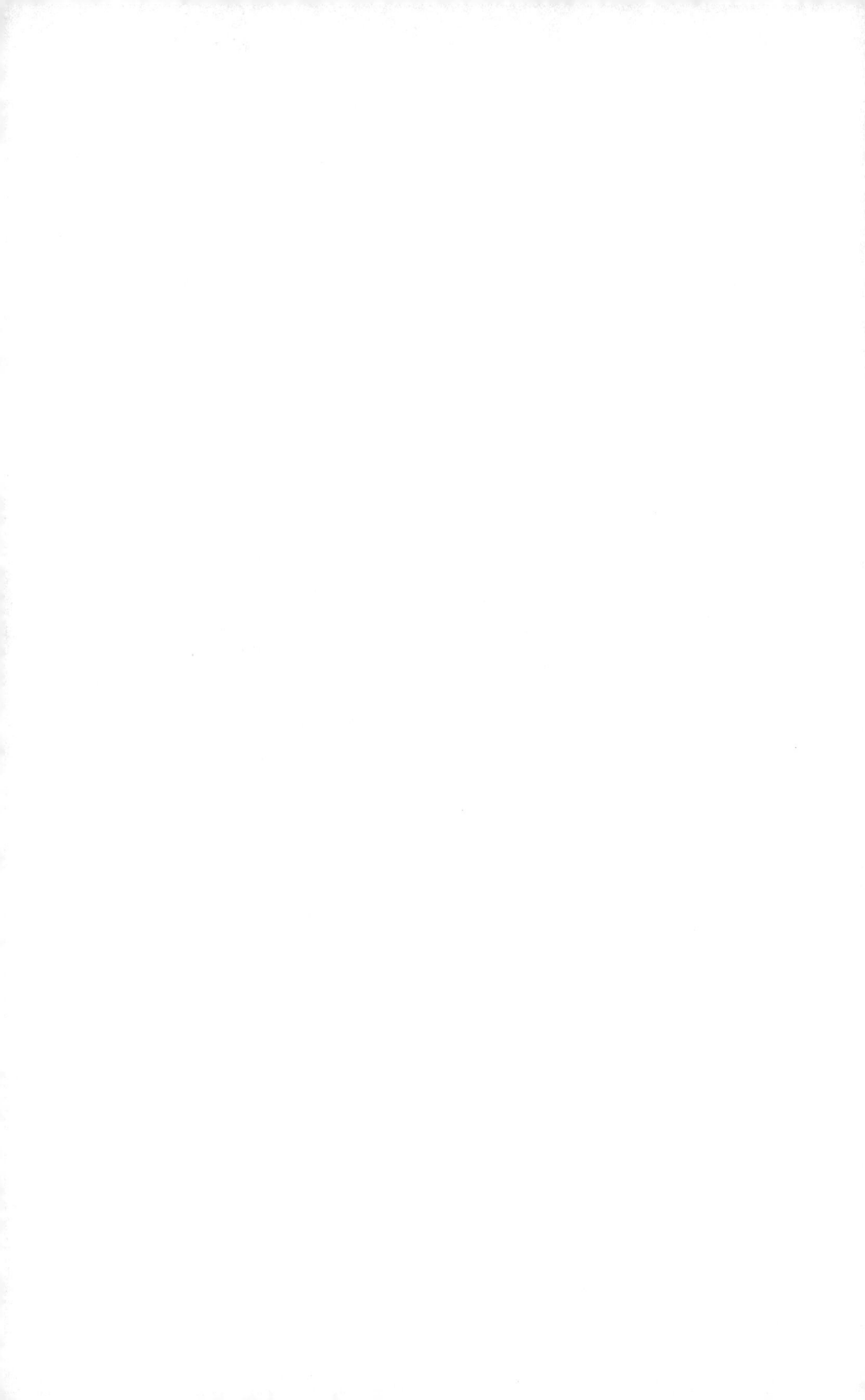

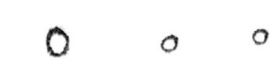

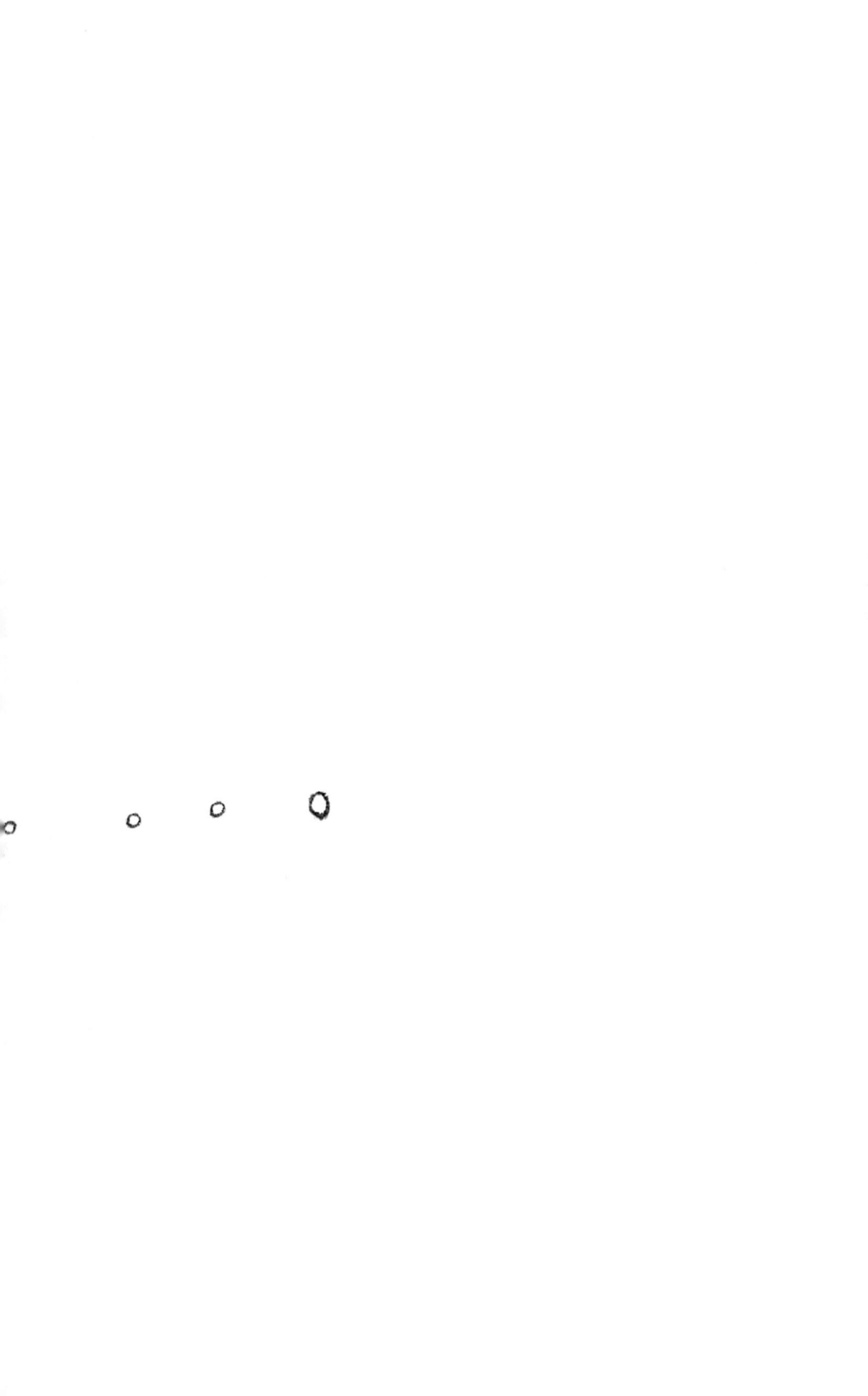

How do you come to it,
the moonlight hunt?

When you pull,
it pulls back.

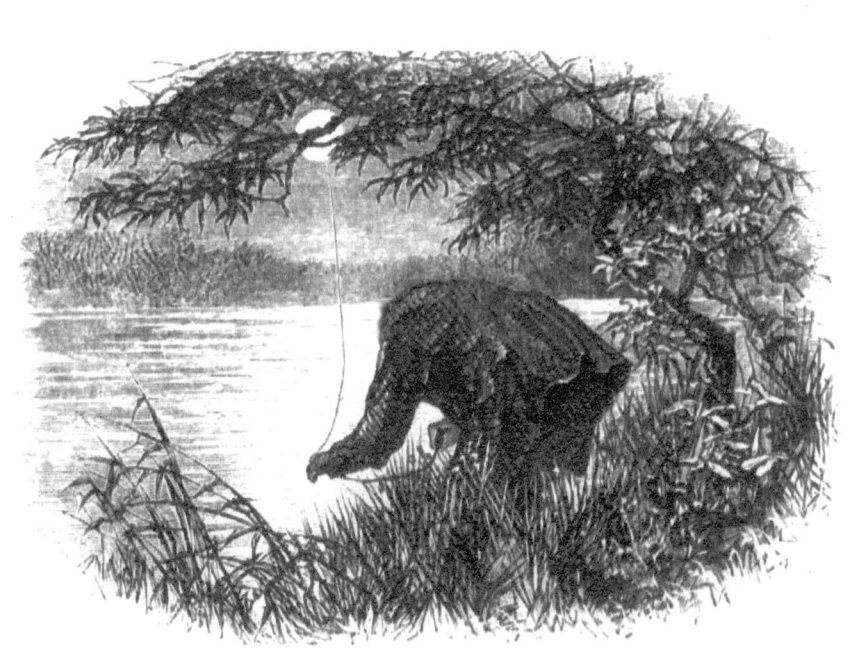

DEDICATION

Images in this text were adapted from illustrations created by Charles Whymper* in 1880. Without that inspiration, this book would not exist.

*Charles Whymper was the brother of Edward Whymper, the mountaineer who led the ill-fated first ascent up the Matterhorn in 1879. Four who followed him never came down the mountain. Edward later illustrated a description of that historic climb, warning his readers to "Climb if you will, but remember that courage and strength are nought without prudence, and that a momentary negligence may destroy the happiness of a lifetime. Do nothing in haste; look well to each step, and from the beginning think what may be the end."

o   o   o

*Pres·ence | ˈprezəns/ | noun | a person or thing that exists or is present in a place but is not seen | or | a place that exists in a person or thing but is not seen.

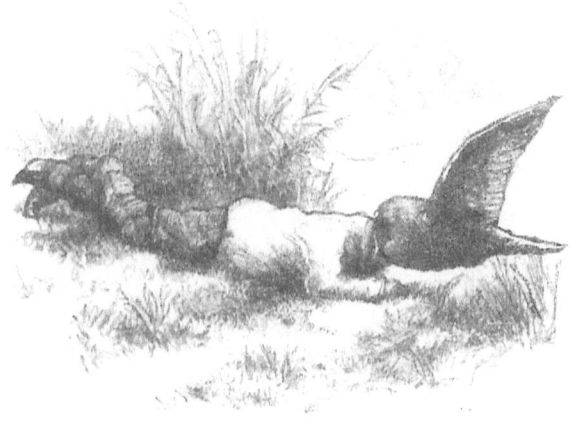